CARL TROTMAN

MULTILEVEL MARKETING

The Complete Guide to Multi Level Marketing Secrets,
Discover All the Valuable Information You Need to
Know About Multi Level Marketing

Descrierea CIP a Bibliotecii Naţionale a României
CARL TROTMAN
   MULTILEVEL MARKETING. The Complete Guide to Multi Level Marketing Secrets, Discover All the Valuable Information You Need to Know About Multi Level Marketing / Carl Trotman. – Bucharest: Editura My Ebook, 2020
   ISBN

CARL TROTMAN

MULTILEVEL MARKETING

The Complete Guide to Multi Level Marketing Secrets, Discover All the Valuable Information You Need to Know About Multi Level Marketing

My Ebook Publishing House
Bucharest, 2020

TABLE OF CONTENT

CHAPTER 1

THE MULTILEVEL MARKETING CONCEPT

What is Multi-Level Marketing?

Multi-level Marketing, or MLM, is a marketing strategy which creates a down line of distributors and a hierarchy of multiple levels of compensation. The sales force is compensated not only for their own sales but also for the sales of the people they help recruit. Firms, having a large product base, often cannot employ equivalent sales force; and believe they would be better off without the traditional approach. Hence, they implement MLM to survive competition from multi-nationals.

MLM is also known as Network Marketing because it utilizes a network of individual customers to hit other potential customers. In other words, every individual customer serves as a sales representative.

Multi-Level Marketing Vs. Pyramid Marketing

People often confuse MLM with pyramid marketing; however there is very clear distinction between the two approaches: pyramid marketing is about getting your money and then using you to recruit other distributors; MLM, on the other hand, is about moving the product through a larger network of distributors so that the business can increase sales volume.

Another difference between MLM and pyramid marketing is that Pyramid marketing requires each level to DOUBLE before a new level is created so it isn't fair to people lower down in the levels and also unethical. MLM, however, awards a commission based upon the volume of product sold through own sales efforts as well as that of the down line organization.

Since MLM faces the risks of initiating a business that has not been tested by the customers is not recognized, people prefer to wait a coupe of years before joining. Hence, they also witness the company's track-record and reliability.

Structure of Multi-Level Marketing

Multi-level Marketing follows a significantly different structure than Pyramid marketing: the network is divided into parts comprising of different number of people. Some parts of the network may comprise of lesser people because the initiator might not have been able to sign-up more people; however, other parts may have flourished due to a hard-working marketing genius have good resources. Hence, MLM turns out to be a fairer approach to income generation.

Growth within Multi-Level Marketing Firms

An MLM opportunity, having a wide-spread network, brings greater growth prospects as members become eager to introduce more people. Furthermore, those present higher up in the network are encouraged to share their experiences with those subordinating them. This is because improvements in the performance of new entrants and subordinates will result in higher profits for the seniors.

Hence, great income-earning opportunities can be availed out of Multi-level Marketing firms. The only key is to select one with a successful product or service; such that you would prefer for yourself.

CHAPTER 2

UNDERSTANDING THE *MLM* SITUATION
AND OPPORTUNITIES

Multi-level Marketing is in fact a Distribution Revolution. The evolution of multi-level marketing has fostered a business paradigm shift that has changed remarkably the traditional ways through which a product was marketed and distributed to the end users. Multi-level marketing has eliminated the need of requiring additional warehouses, wholesalers, and retailers and advertising budgets making it as one of the lowest cost marketing methods. Hence this new mode of marketing has freed up a lot of money that was previously being eaten up by huge advertising budgets and these funds can now be utilized by developing better and innovative products.

Scope of Multi-Level Marketing

The multi-level marketing technique incorporates multiple levels of marketing spreading to masses of potential customers and this is what actually all companies desire that is to reach to maximum number of prospects. Especially with the advent of internet marketing, the scope of MLM or Network Marketing has reached the apex. Companies in various industries like the health care products, beauty and skin care lines, cosmetics, and various others cannot actually survive in the long run without actually implementing Multi-level marketing strategies especially amid the course of their business.

Highlighting the scope of Multi-Level Marketing, Michael L. Sheffield, the CEO of Sheffield Research Network, a Direct selling and MLM consulting firm, in his Direct Sales Journal, issue of Feb / Mar 1999, wrote an article titled "Comp Plan Conversion: Direct Sales to MLM Compensation Plans" in which he maintained that MLM has introduced a paradigm shift in the traditional direct selling business and with the internet revolution the success of MLM companies has raised many folds. He further cited the statement produced by Neil Offen, president of the Direct Selling Association that MLM had gone from 25 percent of Direct Selling Association membership in 1990 to 77.3 percent in 1999.

Multi-level Marketing Opportunities

Multi-level Marketing is a career of uncountable opportunities and growth prospects in the economy. Today multi-level marketing is not only viewed as one of the most cost effective and efficient sources of marketing and distributing your products and enhance your sales, profits and business leads but also it is considered to be a source of employment generation in the economy. As more and more people are moving towards e-marketing and e-selling, MLM is creating a buddle of employment opportunities and is considered to be a source of residual income for a number of people around the world including students, unemployed, and the women especially the house wives. Not only has this, MLM offers a variety of benefits to the companies to achieve maximum profits.

CHAPTER 3

UNDERSTANDING THE *MLM* MODEL

As we have discussed earlier that MLM marketing is also referred to as Network Marketing and as the name implies it has multiple number of people (and/ or networks) marketing a product to the consumers. In very simple words under multiple-level marketing a company employees a sales representative (sometimes referred to as a distributor, an affiliate or an associate) who performs the following basic tasks,

- ❑ Firstly getting customers and generating sales.
- ❑ Secondly generating, recruiting and training other people as sales reps to get customers or generate sales.

Let's discuss in detail how the Multi-Level marketing model works?

Multi-level Marketing Model

The following four step model will demonstrate how a multi-level marketing model works:

> ### *Step I: Sales Representatives gets the customers*

Initially the MLM Company appoints a sales representative and / or distributor whose primary motive is to sell the product or service to the prospective customers. The initial number of customers he has to get varies with the company's plan and commission structure. But it is usually better to get as many customers as the person can retain effectively and can make repeat sales to them. Also if your company's payment structure is more rewarding towards training people to get more customers than as a MLM marketer you should limit your efforts towards getting a few customers first at this stage and than focus on next stage that is getting them trained to promote sales. This strategy is well appropriate for companies who pay you to "duplicate your self".

> *Step II: Train and recruit a person as a sales representative:*

After generating a few customers and making sales to them as done by normal direct marketing or direct sales, a multi-level marketer next job is to train a person to act as sales representative and to convince him to bring more prospects and generate more sales for the company. This person would be called your downline. Here your role is of a recruiter rather than a retailer or distributor.

> *Step III: You teach the rep to train and recruit another person as sales rep:*

Once your sales rep get enough number of customers at will and generates sufficient sales, it is time for you to train them to get a sales rep. Your job as a leader has now multiple dimensions such as generating further sales, training people to become sales rep and training the sales rep to train future people as sales rep. The focus of your efforts will again depends on your commission plan, you as a marketer would off course concentrate your efforts where you can get higher commissions.

> ## *Step IV: Repeat the above steps to generate a chain:*

Once you recruit and train your sales rep to train further people and generate more customers, now you can recruit another sales rep and follow the same procedure making a network of distributors within you downline. This is the reason why it is called multi-level or network marketing and hence companies through MLM tactics cannot only generate reliable customers but also can get its products and/ or services to masses of people with minimal costs and in a relatively shorter period of time as compared to the tradition marketing methods.

The above procedure well explains the MLM model but is it always that easier to get as it appears? Or how is it possible for a company to promote MLM marketing? A well-designed compensation plan is the only answer to the above questions. In our next chapter we will discuss guidelines to develop an effective compensation plan.

CHAPTER 4

TIPS TO DEVELOP APPROPRIATE COMPENSATION PLAN

As we have discussed earlier that Multi Level Marketing is simply a business model for moving products and services from production to the consumer using a network of independent distributors with a multi level commission payout plan. Since distributors can recruit other distributors and establish teams that work together, the pay out plan is a bit complex too. In any MLM company the basic key to drive the MLM marketing force in the required direction to produce the best results is the compensation plan. Commission plans or compensation plans are how MLM companies reward a distributor's production that drives the distribution channel to maximize profits.

Basic Compensation Strategy

It is essential to highlight that every company is different and each has different commission plans, some of which appear complex or complicated too. However the underlying compensation strategy has the following basic components.

- *Retail Commission:* As the name implies retail commission is the commission allocated to motivate the marketer to generate sales. It is the commission that a marketer will be paid on the number of sales he makes to his customers.

- *Sponsor Commission:* The next component of an MLM compensation plan is the commission that is paid to a marketer for the sales generated by its downline hence it requires the marketer to focus on persuading and generating other sales rep for sales promotion. Companies who want to expand their marketing and distribution efforts usually pay better commissions to motivate their marketer to bring more sales reps to the company.

- *Training Commission:* Few companies also pay their marketers to train the sales reps down the line. These marketers basically act as leaders and have adequate experience, knowledge and skills to train the new staff.

In addition to the above components it is also important to mention that MLM is all about leveraged income that is a sales representative not only earn commissions on his own sales but he also earns commission on the sales generated by the people he has introduced, trained and recruit as sales rep. Also it is imperative for marketers to beware of the tactics some times unethically used by a few MLM companies by developing complex compensation plans. In the up coming chapters we will discuss MLM scams and frauds and means to avoid them.

CHAPTER 5

HOW TO FIND A GOOD *MLM* BUSINESS

Although Multi-Level Marketing business has very sound opportunities and prospects of growth and success, however statics reveals that most of the people who enter this endeavor face though hurdle. A study reveals that almost eighty-five percent of the MLM companies fail within the first eighteen months. Hence for a person it is essentially vital to start this business prudently. Listed below are some guidelines to follow:

Step I: INVESTIGATE THE COMPANY

It is critical for the success of a marketer to join a company that is sound and is viable to enter as a Multi-level marketer. Here are few points to consider:

➢ *Start with a well experienced company:*

In order to enter into Multi-level marketing, it is usually wise to start with a well experienced company that has been in the business at least for three years or more. The reason behind is the company itself has surpassed the initial survival phase and now must be in the growth stage increasing your chances of success as a marketer.

➢ *Opt for a Public Limited Company:*

Well known and well established public limited companies are not only safer to enter but also you have high and easy access to the information regarding the company's background, its people and its business and financial strength. It is also recommended to compare the salary or commission with the average sales of the company that will indicate you whether it is a good place to start with.

➢ *Select a member of a business bureau:*

It is always ideal to join a company that is a member of a business bureau or registered with the Direct Selling Association. This will not only ensures the company's reliability but also you can make your complains to these organizations regarding any misconduct by the company.

> ### *Investigate company's track record:*

Essentially important is to look at the company, see how it does business. Is it on ethical grounds? Check out its track record. Find out whether it has a stable track record and identify whether the company's values match up with yours. It is essentially important for long term presence in the Multi-level marketing industry.

Step II: INVESTIGATE THE PRODUCT:

Along with identifying a sound company it is also highly important to know about the product you have to market. Remember your success as a Multi-level marketer ultimately depends on the sales of the product you are offering. Here are few questions to investigate:

> ### *Is the product marketable?*

As a marketer it is important to pick up a product that is highly marketable and has sound qualities and features through which you can promote sales. Also in order to sell products you need to know their features. Sometimes it is essentially important to research and have sufficient knowledge in order to market your self. For example if you are selling some computer software you should have sound knowledge of the technology. Hence before picking up a company a marketer must evaluate these issues.

➢ *Do you your self like the product?*

If you like the product your self, it will be easier for you to market it and hence you can also convince others to become sales representative. Remember multi-level marketing is more of word of mouth marketing, when you like it your self you feel more confident as you know the product is good and you are no making fake promises.

➢ *Is it reasonably priced?*

Naïve marketers often ignore the importance of price which is one of the reasons of their failure in the field. It is essentially important to ensure that your product is well priced and either it has got excessive qualities or is comparatively cheaper to other brands available in the market, otherwise it will be next to impossible for a marketer to generate enough sales.

Also some companies do offer discounts on certain number of sales, you must identify the discounts associated to improve your profits.

➢ *Is the product consumable?*

In order to generate more commission, try to select consumable products, as it raises the chances of repeat sales. In addition to that if your customer likes the product than you can retain him for long term and hence finally can convince him to act as a sale rep, which will ultimately increase our future earnings.

➢ *Is there a demand of the product?*

Never select products that are obsolete, or are excessively available at retail outlets. If your products do not have enough demand you would be wasting your time and efforts for nothing.

Step III: INVESTIGATE THE COMPENSATION PLAN:

The next crucial step is to well understand the compensation plan. As most of the times a multilevel marketer is providing dual service; one as a seller and the other as a recruiter, hence his commission and compensation depends on both. This is why it is important to well understand the company's compensation policies before hand. Here are a few tips:

> ### *Is your compensation based on sales or recruits?*

Remember that it is an illegal practice to pay commission on the number of recruits. So you must identify the compensation plan. This will help you focus your efforts.

> ### *Identify the hidden costs:*

Some companies do require paying some initial money or membership fee to get your self registered as a marketer or sales rep on companies' behalf. Identify whether you will generate enough commissions to cover your initial money paid. Also if the investment is relatively high be careful as some fraudulent companies do ask for paying huge some initially. Always refrain from joining them.

> ### *Do you have to achieve any targets?*

You must find your targets for example how many members do you have to recruit. Some companies require that

28

you sign up a certain amount of people in a given period of time before you will receive payment. Not only that few companies require you to cross target level of sales first before paying you. This may cause problems for new and naïve marketers.

In addition to above there are also few other important points that guarantees your success as a multi- level marketer. These are:

➢ *Training the sales person:*

Some companies do provide training to their sales rep and MLM marketers about the product features and company's profile. Also good companies do train their staff to improve their marketing skills. It is better to select such company especially if you are new in the multi-level marketing industry.

➢ *Active involvement:*

Some companies also offer a discussion forum where you can interact with the other members. It is good for you as during the course of your work a few questions may arise that you need answers to and you want to get suggestions from other people in the same company who can help you resolve your queries and can give you the correct answers you need.

➤ *Take recommendation from the current member:*

Always get in touch with someone who is already a member of the MLM. Ask them their recommendations about the company and their views regarding the way the MLM system works in the company.

➤ *Beware of Scams:*

There are number of fake companies and fake claims. Beware of them. In the upcoming chapters we will discuss in detail about MLM scams, which will help you to protect your self from entering fake companies.

In a nut shell a good company comprises of people who are committed to products that actually help make people's lives better, which see their distributors as their assets and have promising compensation plans that pay well in return of efforts, that train their people and are always there to help their people. Hence if you follow the above important steps, you will be able to select a good MLM company that will guarantee your success as a multi-level marketer.

CHAPTER 6

MULTILEVEL MARKETING VERSUS
TRADITIONAL MARKETING

The advocates of multilevel marketing describe MLM as the more efficient and effective means of marketing and generating leads and sales to your business. But the traditional marketing companies feel reluctant to adopt new network marketing strategies in order to run their business. Also mostly people don't even understand exactly the differences between both the strategies. This is the reason why we have dedicated this chapter to explore difference between the multi level marketing and the traditional marketing strategies.

Lets' explore the major differences:

Difference between MLM and Traditional Marketing

✓ The most significant difference between MLM and the traditional marketing is the role of the marketer. In multi level marketing initially an individual is hired as a sales representative who is required to market the company and its products and / or services and generate sales, which is fairly similar to any traditional marketing business. However on the other hand under multi level marketing, he is also required to identify and recruit additional sales reps as his down line. The new sales rep in turn can appoint another person as company's sales rep or marketer.

✓ Under MLM a marketer has the authority to get customers and recruits and trains another sales person to get customers. However in a traditional marketing company, a sales manager and /or sales reps are hired by the company itself.

✓ Under MLM an unlimited number of sales reps can be hired no matter whether they generate enough sales or not however under a non-MLM company sales reps are hired based on the financial resources of the company. Also a new sales manager is only hired when the existing manager is overwhelmed.

✓ In a MLM company the structure of the distributing network expands vertically, however in a tradition marketing company there is generally horizontal expansion.

✓ The MLM marketers are usually paid commissions, i.e. their compensation is usually based on number of sales made by them or by the people in their down line. This is the reason why MLM enjoys rapid expansion as the marketers can recruit as many sales reps as they like and the company doesn't have to worry about fixed salaries. However, in traditional marketing the sales managers or reps are usually paid fixed salaries.

✓ Also MLM companies usually do not require high set up costs as opposed to the traditional ones that require huge investments to set up a whole marketing and distribution channel.

✓ One of the other major characteristics of multi level marketing is that the parent companies are making plenty of money. Sales force under MLM is so vast that even if no single promoter is selling at high levels but the group as a whole is selling at a very high level, the company would still enjoy the profits. However under traditional set up if a manager is not performing well the sales of the company are adversely affected.

✓ Under MLM the high performers earns high and reach to the top and the rest (the low performers) can not survive and leave the market themselves. The MLM Company like any other traditional company does not have to worry about going through the tedious procedures of appraisals, hiring and firing etc.

Hence the above differences clearly manifests the advantages associated with the multilevel marketing over the traditional marketing methods as MLM is not only the most flexible way of marketing but also due to its network feature it has the tendency of expanding rapidly in the market and if directed effectively it can earn huge profits to the company. Not only that people who can join the marketing team under MLM can work any time they like and reap the benefits on not only the sales they make but also on the sales made by the reps they recruit. Hence MLM has the characteristics of enjoying leveraged income and greater market penetration.

CHAPTER 7

HOW TO IMPROVE YOUR MULTILEVEL MARKETING SKILLS

In this chapter we will discuss a few guidelines that will help you improve your skills as a multi-level marketer. It is essential for a marketer to understand that, no matter how great the company he selects and how demanding the products are, what one must not forget is that multi-level marketing demands hard work and commitment. It is not possible to make huge sums of money just by signing up once and then sit back and wait for the cash to flow in. You need to constantly train and update your self and improve your efforts to ensure long term gains and maximize profits. Here are a few tips that will help you improve your skills as a multi-level marketer.

> *Managing your downline:*

Remember your down line is your asset and a source of your income. Hence it is important to manage your downline properly and keep motivating your downline to produce maximum results and generate maximum sales.

> *Understanding different people:*

It is important for a marketer to understand that he or she is dealing with a number of people at a time, all mostly from different backgrounds. It is essential for him to train each of them appropriately as each may require a different set of information and skill to improve their efficiency. Also in order to convince people to act as sales rep you as a marketer should persuade them according to their needs and level.

> *Learn to accept rejection:*

Multiple-level marketing has a high rate of rejection, hence it is important to stay positive and accept to take 'NO'.

➢ *Keep Focus and be persistent:*

Some people tend to lose interest quickly if they think their plans are not working up to the mark. A multi-level marketer should avoid this as it requires persistency and focused efforts in order to achieve success.

➢ *Undertake constant research:*

Again your success as a marketer highly depends on the company and product you select. Therefore it is imperative to research well before entering into the venture.

➢ *Constantly train and update yourself:*

Try to pick up companies that provide constant training to their marketers, this well help you to keep your self updated. If you understand the latest trends, technologies and the product features well, you are in a better position to persuade customers, generate sales and lead your downline.

> *Improve your communication skills:*

Effective communication and selling skills are keys for the success of every marketer; hence an multi level marketer should constantly improve on his communication skills.

> *Walk the talk- reliability:*

In order to achieve repeat sales, you need to provide reliable information. Hence you should responsibility market your product and avoid unethical ways of generating sales and prospects.

CHAPTER 8

ESSENTIALS OF *MLM* BUSINESS

Thousands of MLM companies are operating in the world today, but most of them vanish with time. New companies keep coming and exiting the market. Only the companies that are great can retain long term existence. It is essentially important to find out which companies are the successful MLM's? What are their characteristics? How a company can ensure success of its MLM strategies. Here are some of highlights of a top-performing Multi-level marketing company.

➤ *Unique Product:*

No matter how effective your business or marketing strategy is and how good is your sales force, nothing works if you're offering is of no worth. A unique and a well developed product that actually satisfies the needs of the customer is a must. Without a quality product that is unique to the market, you can not survive in the market, no matter how big you are.

> ## *Stability:*

The word stability often denotes longevity and endurance in the long run. A well established company has chances to retain short term economic shocks in demands and prices. Also companies that have consistent management plans and policies and defined long term goals demonstrate long term stability and persistence. If the key decisions and decision makers has changed frequently throughout the company's history than its stability is questionable.

> ## *Financial Strength:*

Financial stability and strength is another component that constitutes stability. Before entering into MLM a company must identify that whether it has adequate resources and funds to meet the distributors' compensation. Also companies must identify whether it would be profitable to entail network marketing and does the expected benefits offset the costs associated.

➢ Member Training and Support

The most important feature of a well-performing multi level marketing company is the quality of its training and support for distributors or affiliates. Companies that view their distributors as assets always focus to educate and train their people not only to sharpen their skills but also to enable them to keep abreast with any changes or new trends in the multi level marketing industry. These companies provide constant training through webinars, chat rooms and video conferences to their sales teams. Also successful companies provide different channels to their distributors where they can resolve their queries and concerns such as live chat rooms, resource library, informative and interactive website and distributor support hotlines.

➢ Business Building Tools

It is important to remember that successful marketers are imperative for a company's success. This is the reason why top-performing multi-level marketing companies often provide a variety of effective business building tools to their distributors. Various helpful tools like e-cards, diaries, calendars, customer relationship management systems, freebies, testers, auto responders and various other online resources are provided to their distributors.

➢ *Compensation Plan*

An effective compensation plan is again a must for multi-level marketing success. An effective MLM marketing company knows the significance of its distribution force and offers its distributors a generous and balanced compensation plan. It is also important that irrespective of what compensation model the company is using, the plan must be simple, straight-forward and easy-to-understand and should reward its distributors or affiliates with progressive bonus levels. So that it motivates them to increase their efforts to enhance sales volume, and recruit more qualified prospects.

Hence these are the basic characteristics that ensures survival and success of a Multi-level marketing company, these few features should guide you how to ensure multi-level marketing success.

CHAPTER 9

THE LEGALITY OF MULTI LEVEL MARKETING

Multi-level marketing is a relatively new and complex marketing concept, although it has been practiced since years in one way or another by many companies, but a vast majority of people get it confused with pyramid schemes and questions the legality of multi-level marketing. Now the question is, is MLM legal? Here is the answer: Yes, it is legal.

Until 1979, multi-level marketing was usually considered as scam or illegal as it was never tested and adjudicated in court. In 1975 Amyway Corporation was accused and sued by the US Federal Trade commission for operating as illegal pyramid scheme and after four years of litigation Amyway won the case and the court ruled out that the company's multi-level marketing program is a legitimate business and is not an illegal pyramid scheme. Hence now it is fairly clear that Multi-level marketing is legal and not a scam.

As by now it is clear that multi-level marketing is legal and there is no second thought about this. Although companies who undertake multi-level marketing programs has to strictly develop strategies that fall under the definition of multi level marketing as there is a fine line between multi-level marketing and pyramid marketing which is illegal. Also due to the complexity of the commission structures, companies sometimes develop if not illegal but unethical strategies that is not beneficial for the communities and the general public.

However to legally fall under the Multi-level marketing category, apart from using common sense the following guidelines given by the US Federal Trade Commission (FTC) must be adhered to:

❑ Never enter into any plan that promises commissions for recruiting additional distributors. It is constituted under an illegal pyramid scheme. Your compensation must be linked to the actual sales made by you or your downline not on the number of recruits.

❑ Plans that ask new distributors for making an upfront fee or to purchase expensive inventory are usually skeptical so it is essential to be cautious of them. These plans can collapse quickly and also may be thinly-disguised pyramid schemes.

❏ Also plans that claim that you will make more money by increasing your downline are unrealistic. You are paid commissions on sales made by the people you recruit not only by recruiting more and more reps. So beware of them.

❏ Beware of shills. False or over projected references used by companies to lure you are unrealistic so be cautious.

❏ Remember you do not sell miracles. So engaging with companies that claim to sell miracle products. Also remember that as per the FTC guide lines, a distributor or a marketer is ethically responsible for the promises he made. So don't promise what you can't fulfill.

❏ Never enter into a contract in a high-pressure situation demanding "Now or never". These are all unethical tactics practice by companies to trap you. Always take your time and take advice from friends and other professional people like accountants, lawyers etc to evaluate the viability of the project.

❏ In addition to the above guidelines FTC also requires that the multi level marketing company must derive at least 70% of its income from retail sales to non-distributors. If this criteria is not met than in several cases the courts have concluded the MLM company is in the business of endlessly recruiting distributors who recruit distributors, which may turns these companies into pyramid schemes, not sales and distribution companies.

Hence the above guidelines are important to identify whether the MLM Company falls under the legal definition of doing business. But this is not all; apart from being legal it is essentially important for the multi level marketing Company to use ethical standards and procedures to generate their business and profits. Further in this text we will highlight the general scams and unethical practices that are usually practiced by few MLM companies to deceit their people and the ways to avoid them.

CHAPTER 10

MULTI LEVEL MARKETING SCAMS
AND TIPS TO AVOID THEM

As we have discussed earlier that the success of MLM depends largely on increasing the number of sales through sales representative. Sometimes companies in order to attract people use false claims. This is one of the major reasons why many individuals fear MLM is because they believe they are going to get scammed. If you search the net you will find a lot of examples of companies making fake claims and MLM scam. Here are a few examples how companies use unethical practices to trick people:

- Offering money back guarantee schemes

- Offering miracles instead of real products

- Asking new distributors to pay upfront fee

- Promises to give people down lines once they signup with them

- Sometimes MLM companies do not even exist in reality, they just create false websites to trap individuals

- Demanding you to buy a certain percentage of their product initially, which you might cannot be able to sell and hence incur losses.

- Promising you unreasonably high commissions on your sales.

Apart from them many MLM companies tactically plan there commission scheme that actually takes money away from the marketers or the people working under the network. Naïve marketers usually do not understand that they are being scammed and even after putting hundred percent efforts and generating enough customers they fail to achieve companies' unrealistic targets and can get nothing out of their efforts. This is the reason why it is always essential for a marketer to think prudently and investigate properly before entering into the MLM venture and stay away from the companies which apply unethical tactics to generate profits. Listed below are few tips to avoid scam.

Tips to Avoid Multi level Marketing Scams:

❑ Research the company and its management. For example if you have no access to the company, no phone numbers, addresses, or contact people, then these are the signs that you are being scammed.

❑ Read the policy and procedures before you join. Also take some professionals advice before signing up any agreement.

❑ Avoid lead generation systems that rely on friends and family.

❑ Well understand the compensation plan. Also make sure that you are being compensated for the sales you and your downline generates and not on the number of people you recruit as the later is illegal pyramid scheme.

❑ Investigate whether up line support is available. Identify whether the company invest funds and resources in training their distributors. Only good and reliable companies will invest in training their staff.

❑ If the Multi-level marketing company is asking for several hundreds or thousands to join upfront, there may be chances of being scammed.

❑ Always remember that MLM success takes time and demands hard work, never join companies that promise over night profits.

By following the above tips a naïve marketer can reduce the chances of being scammed and hence focus his efforts in reliable and realistic MLM business.

CHAPTER 11

ONLINE MULTI LEVEL
MARKETING OPPORTUNITIES

So far our discussion was based on understanding the basics of Multi-level marketing and one thing that is obvious through out our discussion is that every multi level marketing company aims at reaching more and more prospects and generating more and more sales. Now just think for a moment in the current era which is the best possible medium for reaching maximum number of prospects investing minimum time and efforts. The answer is quite simple, 'the internet'. MLM companies by going online can transform their business into success and can reach to billions of customers by incorporating online multi-level marketing strategies. Top-rated multilevel marketing companies execute several online marketing strategies in order to generate more and more business leads and then concentrate their marketing efforts on the leads to generate sales.

Guidelines for Efficient Online Multi-level Marketing

Let's explore a few guidelines to make your online MLM business a success;

✓ *Create your Website:*

The first and foremost step to ensure your online presence is to create your website. Every online multi level marketing system starts with a website.

✓ *Attract Visitors:*

No matter how good is your company, your product or your website, its worthless if no ones know about it? Hence the next step is to attract traffic towards your website. Now the question is how to do that? The answer is advertising your-self. This can be done through incorporating various online marketing strategies such as through article marketing, viral marketing, blogging, video marketing, social marketing, sponsored ads like pay-per click etc. In order to generate maximum traffic to your website it is essentially important to use effective key words and develop contents and tactics that maximize your search engine ranking. All these procedures if employed efficiently can bring billions of visitors to your website.

✓ *Generate Leads:*

Once you get traffic to your website it is now the stage where you obtain contact information to build lists of interested prospects. Lead generation and list building is the most important step. Further in this text we will explore in details about ways through which leads can be generated. You can do this through squeeze pages, opt-in email pages, pop-ups etc. Hence in this way you can get information about the person who is interested in your company and in your product and may buy your product in the future.

✓ *Building Relationship:*

Once you generate a lead, its time now to build relationship with the prospect and develop trust and persuade him to buy the product. Staying in touch with your prospect is crucial. This can be done through an auto responder, where you send predefined set of emails to the prospect to build credibility and trust.

✓ *Generate sales:*

Once you do that you can now convince your lead to purchase your product and turn the lead into a customer. Remember to keep in touch with your customer so that he can not only make repeat sales but you can also convince him to join your team and finally recruit him as a sales rep.

By following above guidelines you as a marketer can reap maximum profits and lead to success. However, it is essentially important for a multi-level marketer to develop long term relationship with its customers as it is the key for his long term survival in the MLM industry. In the next chapter we will explore the importance of relationship building.

CHAPTER 12

RELATIONSHIP BUILDING THROUGH MULTILEVEL MARKETING

For every business the key to success is building relationships with you customers. This is also true for any multi level marketing business, in fact the importance of building relation increases two fold in multi level marketing as you as a marketer has not only to retain your customers to generate repeat sales but also building trust with them so that you can convince them to join your team as a marketer and a future sales rep. So how do you build relationships online? Here are the basic tips that you need to follow to build relationships online.

❏ *Bring value to your customers:*

One of the best ways to retain your customers is to provide them value consistently. In multilevel marketing one of the finest ways to bring value to your prospect is to provide them the best product. When your product satisfies the customers, it means that you have meet the promises made to them and hence it develops your credibility and people trust you and will come back to you repeatedly.

Is this it? No, remember we are talking about MLM marketing, where your earnings are based on the sales made by your downline. Hence for a multilevel marketer it is equally important to build healthy and lasting relationships with people in their down lines. Your down lines are your assets. Always try to constantly train, help and satisfy your down lines and always be there to resolve their issues and problems. In this way you can not only raise your own earnings but can increase your company's profits.

□ *Brand your self:*

As a lot of people are doing online multi level marketing business and in order to stand out of your competitors and prove your-self, it is essential to brand your self. The best way to do this is to create your website or a blog that tells people about you. When you do that you increase your credibility and beat your competitors.

❑ *Stay in touch:*

A very common mistake which most of the MLM marketers do is to leave customers once they make sales. Never do that. It is very important to keep in touch with the customer, asking him how he found the product, what else he wants in the product. These tactics will help you retain your customers for long run and ensure repeat sales.

❑ *Be positive:*

Few marketers quickly get upset due to demand fluctuations in the market. It is important as a leader to stay positive and be persistent even you might not produce enough sales. The reason behind if your loose hopes you cannot motivate the people in your downline hence always stay positive and focused.

CHAPTER 13

GENERATING LEADS

Throughout our discussion within this text we have highlighted that a multilevel marketer has to attain two basic goals. One is to sell the products or services of the parent company and the other is to encourage the customer to also become an independent distributor. Both these objectives call for such actions that demands creation of maximum business prospects also known as the business leads.

There are several ways of generating leads. Usually a marketer generates his or her own leads through referrals from friends, family members, and acquaintances. But are that enough? Certainly no. hence the marketer has to use various tools like holding event or trade shows, distributing pamphlets, others may include conducting research or even the marketer can simply buy a list from list building companies or other relevant sources.

Online multi level marketers also use several tactics to generate leads. This can be done through squeeze pages, opt-in email pages, pop-ups etc. These are basically common ways of collecting information from a visitor for example through squeeze page you provide a piece of information in the form of an article or a video clip to the customer and then asking customer to leave his contact details (usually email, mailing address, and other contact info) if he requires further details. In this way you can get information about the person who may buy your product in the future. Hence, if you have an online existence, you are in the position of generating masses of business leads, which are basically your potential customers. Once you get them it will help you maintain long term relationship with them and you can reach out to them to offer yourself, your offerings and your services.

Hence a multi level marketer should generate as many leads as he can that is crucial not only for his existence but also for the company's survival.

CHAPTER 14

MEASURING MULTILEVEL MARKETING PERFORMANCE

An integral part of analyzing the success of the Multi level marketing campaign is to measure the performance of the multi level marketing team. You need to identify the key performance indicators that have remarkable impact on your firm's profitability. These key indicators are basically control points that help you to monitor the progress of your multilevel marketing team and its effects on your business. Due to very complex nature of the network marketing scenario and usually complicated compensation plans, few companies sometimes ignore to evaluate the performance of its team and its overall impact on the business. But is it right or a big blunder? Only an insane would say its right.

Multi level team performance has a vital impact on your business and it is crucial to assess the performance as it will assist you in formulating your future business strategies and multi level marketing business plan. Investing more in the areas which are promising and reducing efforts where there is not much potential. But the question is how do you measure team performance? How can it provide you with helpful data for planning future business strategy? What are the key indicators of performance?

In order to evaluate performance it is essential to identify the key performance indicators. For example identify whether your team achieved the targets given to them, the number of sales made by your team, number of key recruits you get, conducting a cost and benefit analysis, number of repeat sales or repeat customers, increase in sales, satisfaction level of your team, satisfaction level of your customers etc. Once you do that you can utilize these results to develop future business policies. Hence measuring key performance indicators is a well recognized process practiced by almost all large companies to use it as a basis to formulate future strategies.

One of the other important points to consider is to evaluate your business targets. Some companies set unrealistic targets that are highly difficult to achieve. In order to evaluate the actual performance it is also essential to evaluate your compensation plan. For example if there is very low distributor retention than instead of penalizing your team you need to reevaluate your commission plan and identify why your team is unable to produce effective results. Also account for forces that are not in control of your marketers for example an economic down turn, demand short fall etc. Hence in order to ensure longevity MLM companies must constantly evaluate their team performance and took measures to correct any loop holes.

CHAPTER 15

ADVANTAGES OF MULTI-LEVEL MARKETING

Multi level marketing offers a variety of benefits. Listed below are a few advantages associated with MLM business:

> ### *Minimum Entry Barriers:*

Multi level marketing like any other online marketing is an egalitarian industry to get into and it doesn't have any pain staking entry requirements. Also to start your career as a multi-level marketer and to start a MLM business professionally you don't need to be highly qualified, i.e. you can enter into this business without the need of a degree or any particular experience.

➤ *Financial Flexibility:*

Compared to other businesses MLM business relatively has low set-up costs. Although the actual costs vary substantially with the type of compensation plan you offer for example few companies require a substantial monthly investment in the products or services or few requires some additional charges like registration etc to join them as their sales rep or marketer.

➤ *Demands focused efforts:*

The focus of an MLM marketer is just to market the product that is he has to concentrate his efforts in generating sales and sales rep. All the rest is done by the company itself that is you are only marketing an already manufactured product and ones you make a sale you don't have to worry about anything else such as shipping the product to the customer etc.

➤ *Flexible Hours:*

You can run your business at any time you like. You have the flexibility of choosing your work hours. You can work part time, full time, in the evenings, from your home or any where.

Also you do not require a proper office or corporate area to work from.

➢ *MLM offers Leveraged Income:*

One of the major advantages on an MLM business is you basically put initial efforts by training and generating effective sales rep and develop an efficient downline. Once you do that you can reap the profits for the rest of your life. Because generally you are earning compensation or commission on the sales generated by you as well as your downline and the more efficient and hard working your downline the more money you can earn. This is the reason why MLM is usually viewed as a source of leveraged income that is you receive a continuing income from a single initial effort.

➢ *Pre-Existing Systems*

As a MLM marketer you don't need to develop systems to recruit, develop and train your staff. These are taken care of by the company you are representing. All you have to do is to reach to people to market your product and generate sales and to convince people to act as future sales reps.

➢ *Personal Growth and Development:*

MLM marketing is also viewed as an extensive source of personal growth and development of the marketer. Over time you don't only achieve professional selling qualities but MLM helps you to increase your PR and enhance your marketing and leadership qualities.

In the next chapter we will discuss few of disadvantages of multi level marketing.

CHAPTER 16

DISADVANTAGES OF MULTI-LEVEL MARKETING

Having discussed the advantages now let's explores the darker part that is the disadvantages of multilevel marketing. Here is the list:

✓ *Complex Compensation Plans:*

It is important to note that the compensation or commission plans are usually not a simple as they sound. Most of the times companies to keep the MLM financially viable set a number of targets either sales based, performance based or standard based and you are only paid once you achieve these targets. For example few companies pay only if you recruit a specific number of reps to generate future sales, if you fail to achieve this you will not get anything from your sales.

✓ *Financial commitment:*

Few companies trap marketers by asking a number of hidden charges in the form of registration fees, training fees or even some times they charge for the material or marketing tools they provide (for example CD's, broachers, manuals etc) to the marketers for training them about the product and it features and about the company. Most of the times, you will have to commit to purchasing a certain volume of product each month in order to remain eligible to participate in the program. This makes is difficult for you to remain profitable and hinders your long term existence in the industry.

✓ *Demands Extensive Motivation:*

Remember that MLM is all about leveraged income. You can only survive when you earn money from your own sales plus the sales generated through your downline. Hence it is crucially important to keep your downline motivated and focused. Also you need to train and recruit more and more people in order to generate more income. Hence MLM requires continuous efforts and hard work for future survival.

✓ *Severe Competition:*

As MLM business does not require any professional degrees or skills, plus it relatively has no start up or entry barriers, it fosters severe competition. Any one can enter in the market and take away your prospects. This is the reason why to assure longevity; a serious MLM marketer has to really work hard as there are lot others out there ready to work with your sponsors.

CHAPTER 17

WHY MLM GOES WRONG-
THE COMPANY'S PERSPECTIVE

There is so much hype every where about the success of MLM and the financial and other rewards associated by employing a successful MLM campaign. But what are the statistics? What are the real facts? If you do your research you will find out that although several companies associate their success stories to MLM. Big giants like Avon, Amyway, Mary Kay and several others have huge MLM teams which are assets for them. But it is also a truth that almost seventy to eighty percent of the companies that are new entrants in the field encounter failures and loses. Why is it so? Where things go wrong? Here are a few areas that require proper consideration:

Reasons for MLM Failures

Lets' find out a few reasons of MLM failures from a company's perspective:

➤ *Selecting Wrong People:*

One of the major pitfalls is the selection of wrong people. In order to maximize their commissions MLM promoters frequently select any one when recruiting individuals to be part of their down line. People who are actually non serious and if they cannot make enough commissions they portray a bad image of the company every where. This is hazardous for a company's future growth. Other people might feel reluctant to join the company and / or to buy the product.

➤ *Compromising on Research and Development:*

It is also essential for companies to remember that MLM is a part and parcel of your over all business strategy. Few companies focus all their efforts on MLM and forget the rest. This is where things go wrong. With excellent marketing efforts it is also crucial to invest in research and development and producing a unique product with sound features. No matter how good is your marketing and distribution network, without a promising product, all the rest is useless.

➢ *Inflated Commission Plans:*

Some companies, in order to attract more and more people and to stay a head of competitors, offer unrealistic or over inflated commission plans and product prices and promises overnight wealth. Avoid doing that firstly because you may soon collapse financially, secondly you may be viewed as a scam and people feel reluctant to join you.

➢ *Inability to Comprehend Market Demand and Supply:*

In the greed of expanding market penetration and reaching to millions of people, the one major mistake that a few companies do is to forget the basic economics. It is essential to evaluate market demand and supply of the product. Companies may spend huge sums of money in MLM but what they don't realize is the economic scenario. Also the price you fix is a determinant of demand and supply, especially if the product you offer is not too different from what is already available every where in the market. Hence it is essential to evaluate all these factors before investing blindly in MLM.

➤ *Using Unethical Practices:*

The most hazardous move that may damage a company's image is the implementation of unethical practices to generate short term profits. Practices such as making fake promises about product attributes, charging a high up front fee or demanding a huge initial investment from new people to join you distribution team, forcing them to buy huge amount of products that are realistically impossible for them to sell, may earn you short term profits but damage your long term image and existence.

It is true that MLM promises huge sums of money but it is essential to realize that there is no miracle and you need to be prudent and vigilant while developing MLM strategies and should use legitimate and ethical tactics, other wise you will collapse.

CHAPTER 18

SECRETS OF MULTI-LEVEL MARKETING

In the last chapter we discussed reasons behind MLM failures and hence we highlighted a few factors that are essential to consider. Apart from that what MLM companies can do to get maximum benefits out of their multilevel marketing campaign. Are there any MLM secrets to success? How can we stand out of a thousand of competitors already in the market? How can we offer something extra? Here are a few MLM secrets to success:

> ### *Support, support and more support:*

You need to stay at the back of your team. Never leave your MLM team to survive on its own. Keep them updated and educate them about the product, the company and the current market trends and technologies. Remember the survival and success of your team assures the survival of your company.

➤ *Offer something extra*

Good companies always offer a little bit extra to win the trust and loyalty of their employees. Always try to develop relationships with your team. Identify their problems and help them sort them out. Also a few extra bonuses offered to them for example at the time of Christmas or may be sending them on training to improve their marketing skills on company's expenses are the strategies that can foster willingness and loyalty in your team.

➤ *Provide free promotional tools:*

Offering free promotional tools will help you generate more sales. The perks you offer can bring you prospects for example offering freebies which may include free products or services is a remarkable tactic especially if you are offering health products or cosmetic products. You get freebies, which include free products and services.

➢ *Foster team work:*

Multilevel marketing is all about team work and relationship building. It is also beneficial if a company use techniques that foster and team work among the network of its distributors. You can do this by arranging seminars at regular intervals, engaging team members through online chat rooms and other social networks where people can meet up and learn from each other.

➢ *Develop Proper Attitude*

All the MLM marketers should learn the secret of developing proper attitude while they conduct their business especially when you are in online MLM business. As you are not in face to face direct contact with your customer, your attitude should be such to attract your prospect. Respect your prospects and be honest, sincere and polite at all times. Communicate with your prospective buyers in a respectful manner. A good thing to know is, people follow you, once they like you and they will buy from you.

➤ *Never Quit:*

MLM is not a miracle. Most online marketers quit after a few weeks or months. Remember that persistency is a key to success. This is the real secret behind the success of peoples who has made huge sums of money through MLM.

Hence by incorporating these secrets you can offer something extra to your people and your customers and hence reap the profits in the long run.

CHAPTER 19

MULTI-LEVEL MARKETING - AN OVERVIEW

Multi level marketing is an asset for any company who wants to penetrate in the market and generate profits. Every business dreams of getting higher sales so that profits can be earned. By incorporating MLM techniques companies can easily achieve their goals but again it is important to remember that there are no short cuts. Consistency, hard work and efforts are the demands to success.

Although MLM is usually viewed as scam or illegal, but it's not illegal. It is completely legal. However one should beware of the fraudulent practices the less legitimate companies usually employee during the course of their business. Also genuine MLM companies should strictly follow the legal guidelines and employee ethical means of practices that do not only guarantee success but also long term persistence of the firm.

The other dimension of MLM is its extreme flexibility making it possible for many people around to involve in the business and generate money at their own pace. One thing that every Multi level marketer should understand that it is not a miracle and it requires time and efforts to attain success ultimately, so never get upset from initial failures and never give up quickly. Keep going and keep working hard and you are not far from success and reaping huge incomes.

Printed by Libri Plureos GmbH in Hamburg, Germany